hey dad!

hey dad!

words of wisdom on fatherhood

edited by sean keogh

Published in the United States in 2008
by Tangent Publications
an imprint of
Axis Publishing Limited
8c Accommodation Road
London NW11 8ED
www.axispublishing.co.uk

Creative Director: Siân Keogh
Production Manager: Jo Ryan

ISBN 978-1-904707-67-7

9 8 7 6 5 4 3 2 1

Printed and bound in China

about this book

A collection of wit and wisdom based on the theme of fatherhood. Written by and for dads and their children of all ages, it offers a witty, wry, and poignant look at what it means to be a father, how to face the challenges, revel in the delights, and generally pass on the wisdom of other fathers, sons, and daughters.

These remarkable thoughts and sayings are full of joy, anticipation, fulfilment, and goodwill. They have been drawn together from real dads and their families and friends. The sayings are complemented by a series of amusing animal photographs and are guaranteed to inspire.

This is an ideal gift book for fathers and fathers-to-be as a reminder of this unique and special relationship.

about the author

Sean Keogh has worked in publishing for several years, on a variety of books and magazines covering a wide range of subjects. From the many hundreds of contributions that were sent to him by parents and their children from all over the world, he has selected those that best sum up what fatherhood is all about.

A rich man is one whose children run into his arms when his hands are empty.

Dads want to stop you making mistakes, but still let you find your own way.

There's a special place in heaven for a dad who takes his daughter shopping.

Fathers are the powers that be.

We don't need to speak to understand each other perfectly.

It is not flesh and blood
but the heart which makes
us fathers and sons.

It's easy for a father to hear himself talking.

All he has to do is listen to his children!

A dad is a man who expects his son to be as good a man as he meant to be.

By the time a man realizes that maybe his father was right, he usually has a son who thinks he's wrong.

There are three stages of a dad's life—he believes in Santa Claus, he doesn't believe in Santa Claus, he is Santa Claus.

Dads—they say little,
but give a lot.

Q: What do you give the man who doesn't want anything?

A: Anything—he won't mind.

Whatever else you do in life, being a dad makes you most proud.

A father is not so much a father as a walking encyclopedia.

Dad, you're sooooo embarrassing…

…but, I love you.

A man never stands
as tall as when he
kneels to help a child.

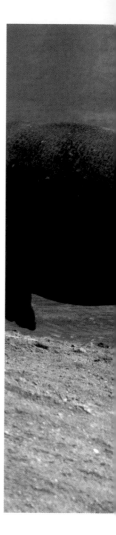

I'm just as lucky as I can be, for the world's coolest dad belongs to me.

Any man can be a father. It takes someone special to be a dad.

To become a father is not hard. To be a father, however, is.

Blessed indeed is
the man who hears
many gentle voices
call him father.

It is a wise father who knows his own child.

One father is worth
more than
a hundred
schoolmasters.

Dad taught me
everything I know.
Unfortunately,
he didn't teach
me everything
he knows.

A dad is someone you look up to, no matter how tall you are.

Fathers send their
sons to college
either because they
went to college,
or because
they didn't.

I cannot think of any need in childhood as strong as the need for a father's protection.

A man's children and his garden both reflect the amount of weeding done during the growing season.

Fathers represent another
way of looking at life.

When you teach your son,
you teach your son's son.

What a dad teaches
at odd moments is more
important than what he
teaches when he's
trying to teach.

You never grow out of
needing your dad.

Think big thoughts but
relish small pleasures.

If you want to keep
your kids, let them go.

Being a dad is a privilege.

Dads hand their kids
the script for life.

If your children look
up to you, you've
made a success of
life's biggest job.

The sooner you treat
your son like a man,
the sooner he will be one.

It's only when you move away that you can measure your father's greatness and fully appreciate it.

To give your best is to
receive the best.

You're a superhero, Dad.

Nothing you have done for
me has ever been wasted.

Dad, you've been everything to me: playmate, friend, and teacher.

Dads help you color between the lines, and tie your shoes.

The word dad is
another word for love.

Dad, you taught
me two words that
mean everything:
care and share.

Dad, your friendship isn't a big thing—it's a million little things.

My love for you is deep
as the ocean.

Dad isn't perfect,
but he's perfect for me.

The only man a girl
can rely on is her dad.

Dad: a son's first hero,
a daughter's first love.

A family without a father
is like a house
without a roof.

A dad is an affectionate encyclopedia.

Dad lets you eat ice-cream
for breakfast…

…but only if mom isn't there.

Children are poor

men's riches.

The most important thing
a father can do for his children
is to love their mother.

Dad is the boss in the house; mom is just the decision maker.

Never lend your
car to anyone
to whom you
are a dad.

The best inheritance you
can leave your kids is
a good example.

The poorest man can leave his children the richest inheritance.

Dad, you taught me
right from wrong.